CW00821276

My Veggie Keto Air Fryer Cookbook

A Complete Veggie Recipe Collection to Improve Your Health

Lucy Grant

Table of Contents

Introduction

What's the difference between an air fryer and deep fryer? Air fryers bake food at a high temperature with a high-powered fan, while deep fryers cook food in a vat of oil that has been heated up to a specific temperature. Both cook food quickly, but an air fryer requires practically zero preheat time while a deep fryer can take upwards of 10 minutes. Air fryers also require little to no oil and deep fryers require a lot that absorb into the food. Food comes out crispy and juicy in both appliances, but don't taste the same, usually because deep fried foods are coated in batter that cook differently in an air fryer vs a deep fryer. Battered foods needs to be sprayed with oil before cooking in an air fryer to help them color and get crispy, while the hot oil soaks into the batter in a deep fryer. Flour-based batters and wet batters don't cook well in an air fryer, but they come out very well in a deep fryer.

The ketogenic diet is one such example. The diet calls for a very small number of carbs to be eaten. This means food such as rice, pasta, and other starchy vegetables like potatoes are off the menu. Even relaxed versions of the keto diet minimize carbs to a large extent and this compromises the goals of many dieters. They end up having to exert large amounts of willpower to follow the diet. This doesn't do them any favors since willpower is like a muscle. At some point, it tires and this is when the dieter goes right back to their old pattern of eating. I have personal experience with this. In terms of health benefits, the keto diet offers the most. The reduction of carbs forces your body to mobilize fat and this results in automatic fat loss and better health.

Feel free to mix and match the recipes you see in here and play around with them. Eating is supposed to be fun! Unfortunately, we've associated fun eating with unhealthy food. This doesn't have to be the case. The air fryer, combined with the Mediterranean diet, will make your mealtimes fun-filled again and full of taste. There's no grease and messy cleanups to deal with anymore. Are you excited yet?

You should be! You're about to embark on a journey full of air fried goodness!

Roasted Squash with Goat Cheese

Prep + Cook Time: 30 minutes

2 Servings

INGREDIENTS

1 lb butternut squash, cut into wedges

½ tsp dried rosemary

2 tbsp olive oil

1 tbsp maple syrup

1 cup goat cheese, crumble

Salt to season

DIRECTIONS

Preheat air fryer to 350 F.

Brush the squash with olive oil and season with salt and rosemary.

Place in the frying basket and Bake for 20 minutes, flipping once halfway through.

Top with goat cheese and drizzle with maple syrup.

Serve warm.

enjoy!

Indian Aloo Tikki

Prep + Cook Time: 30 minutes

2 Servings

INGREDIENTS

4 boiled potatoes, shredded

3 tbsp lemon juice

1 roasted bell pepper, chopped

Salt and black pepper to taste

2 onions, chopped

¼ cup fennel, chopped

5 tbsp flour

2 tbsp ginger-garlic paste

1 tbsp mint leaves, chopped

1 tbsp fresh cilantro, chopped

DIRECTIONS

Preheat your air fryer to 360 F.

In a bowl, mix cilantro, mint, fennel, ginger-garlic paste, flour, salt, and lemon juice.

Add in potatoes, bell pepper, and onions, and mix to combine.

Make the mixture into balls and flatten them to form patties.

Place into the greased frying basket and Bake for 15 minutes, flipping once.

Serve with mint chutney.

enjoy!

Root Vegetable Medley

Prep + Cook Time: 30 minutes

4 Servings

INGREDIENTS

8 shallots, halved

2 carrots, sliced

1 turnip, cut into chunks

1 rutabaga, cut into chunks

2 potatoes, cut into chunks

1 beet, cut into chunks

Salt and black pepper to taste

2 tbsp fresh thyme, chopped

2 tbsp olive oil

2 tbsp tomato pesto

DIRECTIONS

Preheat air fryer to 400 F.

In a bowl, combine all the root vegetables, salt, pepper, and olive oil.

Toss to coat and transfer to the frying basket.

AirFry for 10 minutes, then shake and continue cooking for another 10 minutes.

Combine the pesto with 2 tbsp of water and drizzle over the vegetables, sprinkle with thyme, and serve enjoy!

Cashew & Chickpea Balls

Prep + Cook Time: 30 minutes

4 Servings

INGREDIENTS

2 tbsp olive oil

2 tbsp soy sauce

1 tbsp flax meal

2 cups cooked chickpeas

½ cup sweet onions, chopped

½ cup carrots, grated

½ cup cashews, roasted

Juice of 1 lemon

½ tsp turmeric

1 tsp cumin

1 tsp garlic powder

1 cup rolled oats

DIRECTIONS

Combine olive oil, sweet onions, and carrots in a baking dish and Bake in the air fryer for 6 minutes at 350 F.

Ground the oats and cashews in a food processor.

Remove to a large bowl.

Process the chickpeas with the lemon juice and soy sauce in the food processor until smooth.

Add them to the cashew bowl as well.

Add onions and carrots to the same bowl.

Stir in the remaining ingredients, and mix well.

Make meatballs out of the mixture.

Place the balls in the greased frying basket and Bake for 12 minutes to 370 F, shaking once, until nice and crispy.

Serve warm.

enjoy!

Halloumi Cheese with Veggies

Prep + Cook Time: 15 minutes

4 Servings

INGREDIENTS

6 oz halloumi cheese, cubed

2 zucchinis, cut into even chunks

1 carrot, cut into chunks

1 eggplant, peeled, cut into chunks

2 tsp olive oil

1 tsp dried mixed herbs

Salt and black pepper to taste

DIRECTIONS

In a bowl, add halloumi, zucchinis, carrot, eggplant, olive oil, herbs, salt, and pepper.

Transfer to the frying basket and AirFry for 14 minutes at 340 F, shaking once.

Top with mixed herbs to serve. enjoy!

Quinoa & Veggie Stuffed Peppers

Prep + Cook Time: 30 minutes

2 Servings

INGREDIENTS

1 cup cooked quinoa

2 red bell peppers, cored and cleaned

½ onion, diced

½ cup tomatoes, diced

¼ tsp smoked paprika

Salt and black pepper to taste

1 tsp olive oil

¼ tsp basil

DIRECTIONS

Preheat air fryer to 350 F.

In a bowl, combine quinoa, onion, basil, diced tomatoes, paprika, salt, and pepper and stir.

Stuff the peppers with the filling and brush them with olive oil.

Place the peppers in a greased baking dish and Bake in the fryer for 12 minutes.

Serve warm enjoy!

Chickpea & Spinach Casserole

Prep + Cook Time: 20 minutes

4 Servings

INGREDIENTS

2 tbsp olive oil 1 onion, chopped

Salt and black pepper to taste

2 garlic cloves, minced

1 can coconut milk

1 tbsp ginger, minced

1 lb spinach

½ cup dried tomatoes, chopped

1 14-oz can chickpeas, drained

1 chili pepper, minced

DIRECTIONS

Heat olive oil in a saucepan over medium heat and sauté onion, garlic, chili pepper, ginger, salt, and pepper for 3 minutes.

Add in spinach and stir for 3-4 minutes until wilted.

Transfer to a baking dish.

Mix in the remaining ingredients.

Preheat air fryer to 370 F.

Place the baking dish in the air fryer.

Bake for 15 minutes until golden on top.

Serve warm enjoy!

Southern-Style Corn Cakes

Prep + Cook Time:25 minutes

4-6 Servings

INGREDIENTS

2 cups corn kernels, canned, drained

2 eggs, lightly beaten

⅓ cup green onions, finely chopped

¼ cup parsley, chopped

1 cup flour

½ tsp baking powder

Salt and black pepper to taste

DIRECTIONS

In a bowl, add corn kernels, eggs, parsley, and green onions, and season with salt and pepper; mix well.

Sift flour and baking powder into the bowl and stir.

Line the frying basket with parchment paper and spoon batter dollops, making sure they are separated by at least one inch.

Bake for 10 minutes at 400 F, turning once halfway through.

Serve with sour cream. enjoy!

Balsamic Brussels Sprouts

Preparation Time: 10 minutes

Cooking Time: 20 minutes

Serve: 4

Ingredients:

1 lb brussels sprouts, cut in half

1 small onion, sliced

3 bacon slices, cut into pieces

1 tsp garlic powder

2 tbsp fresh lemon juice

2 tbsp balsamic vinegar

3 tbsp olive oil

1/2 tsp sea salt

Directions:

In a small bowl, whisk together balsamic vinegar, olive oil, lemon juice, garlic powder, and salt.

Toss brussels sprouts with 3 tablespoons of the balsamic vinegar mixture.

Place the cooking tray in the air fryer basket.

Select Air Fry mode.

Set time to 20 minutes and temperature 370 F then press START.

The air fryer display will prompt you to ADD FOOD once the temperature is reached then add brussels sprouts in the air fryer basket.

After 10 minutes toss Brussels sprouts and top with bacon and onion and air fry for 10 minutes more.

Drizzle remaining balsamic vinegar mixture over brussels sprouts and serve.

Parmesan Zucchini Noodles

Preparation Time: 10 minutes

Cooking Time: 10 minutes

Serve: 2

Ingredients:

4 cups zucchini noodles

1/2 cup parmesan cheese, grated

2 tbsp mayonnaise

Directions:

Add zucchini noodles into the microwave-safe bowl and microwave for 3 minutes.

Pat dry zucchini noodles with a paper towel.

In a mixing bowl, toss zucchini noodles with parmesan cheese and mayonnaise.

Place the cooking tray in the air fryer basket.

Line air fryer basket with parchment paper.

Select Air Fry mode.

Set time to 10 minutes and temperature 400 F then press START.

The air fryer display will prompt you to ADD FOOD once the temperature is reached then add zucchini noodles onto the parchment paper in the air fryer basket.

Stir zucchini noodles halfway through.

Serve and enjoy.

Baked Brussels Sprouts

Preparation Time: 10 minutes

Cooking Time: 35 minutes

Serve: 6

Ingredients:

2 cups Brussels sprouts, halved

1/4 tsp garlic powder

1/4 cup olive oil

1/2 tsp cayenne pepper

1/4 tsp salt

Directions:

Add all ingredients into the large bowl and toss well.

Select Bake mode.

Set time to 35 minutes and temperature 400 F then press START.

The air fryer display will prompt you to ADD FOOD once the temperature is reached then add brussels sprouts in the air fryer basket.

Serve and enjoy.

Rosemary Mushrooms

Preparation Time: 10 minutes

Cooking Time: 14 minutes

Serve: 4

Ingredients:

1 lb mushroom caps

1/2 tsp ground coriander

1 tsp rosemary, chopped

1/2 tsp garlic powder

Pepper

Salt

Directions:

Add all ingredients into the mixing bowl and toss well.

Select Air Fry mode.

Set time to 14 minutes and temperature 350 F then press START.

The air fryer display will prompt you to ADD FOOD once the temperature is reached then add mushrooms in the air fryer basket.

Serve and enjoy.

Asian Green Beans

Preparation Time: 10 minutes

Cooking Time: 10 minutes

Serve: 2

Ingredients:

8 oz green beans, trimmed and cut in half

1 tbsp tamari

1 tsp sesame oil

Directions:

Add all ingredients into the large bowl and toss well.

Select Air Fry mode.

Set time to 10 minutes and temperature 350 F then press START.

The air fryer display will prompt you to ADD FOOD once the temperature is reached then add green beans in the air fryer basket.

Stir halfway through. Serve and enjoy.

Roasted Cauliflower Cherry Tomatoes

Preparation Time: 10 minutes

Cooking Time: 20 minutes

Serve: 4

Ingredients:

4 cups cauliflower florets

3 tbsp olive oil

1/2 cup cherry tomatoes, halved

2 tbsp fresh parsley, chopped

2 garlic cloves, sliced

1 tbsp capers, drained

Pepper

Salt

Directions:

In a bowl, toss together cherry tomatoes, cauliflower, oil, garlic, capers, pepper, and salt and spread in baking dish.

Select Bake mode.

Set time to 20 minutes and temperature 400 F then press START.

The air fryer display will prompt you to ADD FOOD once the temperature is reached then place the baking dish in the air fryer basket.

Serve and enjoy.

Air Fry Baby Carrots

Preparation Time: 10 minutes

Cooking Time: 12 minutes

Serve: 4

Ingredients:

3 cups baby carrots

1 tbsp olive oil

Pepper

Salt

Directions:

Add carrots, oil, pepper, and salt into the mixing bowl and toss well. Select Bake mode.

Set time to 12 minutes and temperature 390 F then press START.

The air fryer display will prompt you to ADD FOOD once the temperature is reached then add baby carrots in the air fryer basket.

Stir halfway through. Serve and enjoy.

Broccoli Fritters

Preparation Time: 10 minutes

Cooking Time: 30 minutes

Serve: 4

Ingredients:

2 eggs, lightly beaten

2 garlic cloves, minced

3 cups broccoli florets, steam & chopped

1 cup cheddar cheese, shredded

1 cup mozzarella cheese, shredded

1/4 cup almond flour

Pepper

Salt

Directions:

Add all ingredients into the large bowl and mix until well combined.

Make patties from the broccoli mixture.

Select Bake mode.

Set time to 30 minutes and temperature 375 F then press START.

The air fryer display will prompt you to ADD FOOD once the temperature is reached then place broccoli patties in the air fryer basket.

Serve and enjoy.

Roasted Veggies

Preparation Time: 10 minutes

Cooking Time: 30 minutes

Serve: 6

Ingredients:

1 bell pepper, cut into strips

2 zucchini, sliced

2 tomatoes, quartered

1 eggplant, sliced

1 onion, sliced

5 fresh basil leaves, sliced

2 tsp Italian seasoning

2 tbsp olive oil

Pepper

Salt

Directions:

Add all ingredients except basil leaves into the mixing bowl and toss well.

Select Roast mode.

Set time to 30 minutes and temperature 400 F then press START.

The air fryer display will prompt you to ADD FOOD once the temperature is reached then place vegetable mixture in the air fryer basket.

Stir halfway through.

Garnish with basil and serve.

Delicious Ratatouille

Preparation Time: 10 minutes

Cooking Time: 15 minutes

Serve: 6

Ingredients:

1 eggplant, diced

1 tbsp vinegar

1 onion, diced

3 tomatoes, diced

2 bell peppers, diced

1 1/2 tbsp olive oil

2 tbsp herb de Provence

3 garlic cloves, chopped

Pepper

Salt

Directions:

Add all ingredients into the bowl and toss well and transfer into the baking dish.

Select Air Fry mode.

Set time to 15 minutes and temperature 400 F then press START.

The air fryer display will prompt you to ADD FOOD once the temperature is reached then place the baking dish in the air fryer basket.

Stir halfway through.

Serve and enjoy.

Spiced Green Beans

Preparation Time: 10 minutes

Cooking Time: 10 minutes

Serve: 2

Ingredients:

2 cups green beans

1/8 tsp cayenne pepper

1/8 tsp ground allspice

1/4 tsp ground cinnamon

1/2 tsp dried oregano

2 tbsp olive oil

1/4 tsp ground coriander

1/4 tsp ground cumin

1/2 tsp salt

Directions:

Add all ingredients into the mixing bowl and toss well.

Select Air Fry mode.

Set time to 10 minutes and temperature 370 F then press START.

The air fryer display will prompt you to ADD FOOD once the temperature is reached then add green beans in the air fryer basket.

Stir Halfway through.

Serve and enjoy.

Parmesan Baked Zucchini

Preparation Time: 10 minutes

Cooking Time: 35 minutes

Serve: 6

Ingredients:

2 1/2 lbs zucchini, cut into quarters

1/2 cup parmesan cheese, shredded

6 garlic cloves, crushed

10 oz cherry tomatoes cut in half

1/2 tsp black pepper

1/3 cup parsley, chopped

1 tsp dried basil

3/4 tsp salt

Directions:

Add all ingredients except parsley into the large mixing bowl and stir well to combine.

Pour egg mixture into the greased baking dish.

Select Bake mode. Set time to 35 minutes and temperature 350 F then press START.

The air fryer display will prompt you to ADD FOOD once the temperature is reached then place the baking dish in the air fryer basket.

Serve and enjoy.

Cheese Broccoli Stuffed Pepper

Preparation Time: 10 minutes

Cooking Time: 25 minutes

Serve: 4

Ingredients:

4 eggs

2.5 oz cheddar cheese, grated

2 medium bell peppers, cut in half and deseeded

2 tbsp olive oil

1/4 cup baby broccoli florets

1/4 cup cherry tomatoes

1 tsp dried sage

7 oz unsweetened almond milk

Pepper

Salt

Directions:

In a bowl, whisk together eggs, milk, broccoli, cherry tomatoes, sage, pepper, and salt.

Add olive oil to the baking dish.

Place bell pepper halves in the baking dish.

Pour egg mixture into the bell pepper halves.

Sprinkle cheese on top of bell pepper.

Select Bake mode.

Set time to 25 minutes and temperature 390 F then press START.

The air fryer display will prompt you to ADD FOOD once the temperature is reached then place the baking dish in the air fryer basket.

Serve and enjoy.

Beans with Mushrooms

Preparation Time: 10 minutes

Cooking Time: 25 minutes

Serve: 4

Ingredients:

2 cups mushrooms, sliced

2 tsp garlic, minced

2 cups green beans, clean and cut into pieces

1/4 cup olive oil

1 tsp black pepper

1 tsp sea salt

Directions:

In a bowl, mix together olive oil, pepper, garlic, and salt.

Pour olive oil mixture over green beans and mushrooms and stir to coat.

Spread green beans and mushroom mixture into the baking dish.

Select Bake mode.

Set time to 25 minutes and temperature 400 F then press START.

The air fryer display will prompt you to ADD FOOD once the temperature is reached then place the baking dish in the air fryer basket.

Serve and enjoy.

Tasty Baked Cauliflower

Preparation Time: 10 minutes

Cooking Time: 45 minutes

Serve: 2

Ingredients:

1/2 cauliflower head, cut into florets

2 tbsp olive oil

For seasoning:

1/2 tsp garlic powder

1 tsp onion powder

1 tbsp ground cayenne pepper

2 tbsp ground paprika

1/2 tsp ground cumin

1/2 tsp black pepper

1/2 tsp white pepper

2 tsp salt

Directions:

In a large bowl, mix together all seasoning ingredients.

Add oil and stir well.

Add cauliflower to the bowl seasoning mixture and stir well to coat.

Transfer the cauliflower florets into the baking dish.

Select Bake mode.

Set time to 45 minutes and temperature 400 F then press START.

The air fryer display will prompt you to ADD FOOD once the temperature is reached then place the baking dish in the air fryer basket.

Serve and enjoy

Squash Noodles

Preparation Time: 10 minutes

Cooking Time: 25 minutes

Serve: 2

Ingredients:

1 medium butternut squash, peel and spiralized

3 tbsp cream

1/4 cup parmesan cheese

1 tsp thyme, chopped

1 tbsp sage, chopped

1 tsp garlic powder

2 tbsp cream cheese

Directions:

In a bowl, mix together cream cheese, parmesan, thyme, sage, cream, and garlic powder.

Add noodles to a baking dish. Select Bake mode.

Set time to 20 minutes and temperature 400 F then press START.

The air fryer display will prompt you to ADD FOOD once the temperature is reached then place the baking dish in the air fryer basket.

Spread the cream cheese mixture over noodles and bake for 5 minutes more.

Serve and enjoy.

Roasted Carrots

Preparation Time: 10 minutes

Cooking Time: 35 minutes

Serve: 6

Ingredients:

16 small carrots

1 tbsp fresh parsley, chopped

1 tbsp dried basil

6 garlic cloves, minced

4 tbsp olive oil

1 1/2 tsp salt

Directions:

In a bowl, combine together oil, carrots, basil, garlic, and salt.

Spread the carrots into a baking dish.

Select Bake mode.

Set time to 35 minutes and temperature 375 F then press START.

The air fryer display will prompt you to ADD FOOD once the temperature is reached then place the baking dish in the air fryer basket.

Garnish with parsley and serve.

Cheddar Cheese Broccoli

Preparation Time: 10 minutes

Cooking Time: 30 minutes

Serve: 6

Ingredients:

4 cups broccoli florets

1/4 cup ranch dressing

1/4 cup heavy whipping cream

1/2 cup cheddar cheese, shredded

Pepper

Salt

Directions:

Add all ingredients into the mixing bowl and mix until well coated.

Spread broccoli in baking dish.

Select Bake mode.

Set time to 30 minutes and temperature 375 F then press START.

The air fryer display will prompt you to ADD FOOD once the temperature is reached then place the baking dish in the air fryer basket.

Serve and enjoy.

Baked Artichoke Spinach

Preparation Time: 10 minutes

Cooking Time: 20 minutes

Serve: 3

Ingredients:

6 oz artichoke hearts, chopped

4 oz cream cheese

1/8 tsp red pepper flakes

10 oz baby spinach

1 garlic clove, minced

1 tbsp olive oil

2 oz brie cheese

1/3 cup black olives

Pepper

Salt

Directions:

Heat olive oil in a large pan over medium heat.

Add garlic and sauté for 1-2 minutes.

Add spinach, red pepper flakes, pepper, and salt and cook for 2-3 minutes or until spinach wilted.

Add cream cheese and cook until cheese is melted.

Add artichoke hearts and reduce heat.

Cook for 3-5 minutes more.

Stir in olives.

Transfer mixture to a baking dish and top with cheese.

Select Bake mode.

Set time to 20 minutes and temperature 350 F then press START.

The air fryer display will prompt you to ADD FOOD once the temperature is reached then place the baking dish in the air fryer basket.

Serve and enjoy.

Cheesy Baked Zoodle

Preparation Time: 10 minutes

Cooking Time: 35 minutes

Serve: 4

Ingredients:

2 medium zucchini, spiralized

2 tbsp butter

1 tsp fresh thyme, chopped

1 small onion, sliced

1 cup Fontina cheese, grated

2 tsp Worcestershire sauce

1/4 cup vegetable broth

Pepper

Salt

Directions:

Melt butter in a pan over medium heat.

Add the onion in a pan and sauté for a few minutes.

Add thyme, Worcestershire sauce, pepper, and salt.

Stir for minutes.

Add broth in the pan and cook onions for 10 minutes.

In a large bowl, combine together zucchini noodles and onion mixture and pour into the greased baking dish.

Top with grated cheese.

Select Bake mode.

Set time to 25 minutes and temperature 400 F then press START.

The air fryer display will prompt you to ADD FOOD once the temperature is reached then place the baking dish in the air fryer basket.

Garnish with thyme and serve.

Roasted Cauliflower and Broccoli

Preparation Time: 10 minutes

Cooking Time: 20 minutes

Serve: 6

Ingredients:

4 cups broccoli florets

4 cups cauliflower florets

2/3 cup parmesan cheese, shredded

1/3 cup olive oil

3 garlic cloves, minced

Pepper

Salt

Directions:

Add half parmesan cheese, broccoli, cauliflower, garlic, oil, pepper, and salt into the large bowl and toss well.

Spread broccoli and cauliflower mixture in a baking dish.

Select Bake mode.

Set time to 20 minutes and temperature 400 F then press START.

The air fryer display will prompt you to ADD FOOD once the temperature is reached then place the baking dish in the air fryer basket.

Add remaining cheese and toss well.

Serve and enjoy.

Delicious Spaghetti Squash

Preparation Time: 10 minutes

Cooking Time: 10 minutes

Serve: 4

Ingredients:

2 cups spaghetti squash, cooked and drained

4 oz mozzarella cheese, cubed

1/4 cup basil pesto

1/2 cup ricotta cheese

1 tbsp olive oil

Pepper

Salt

Directions:

In a bowl, combine together olive oil and squash.

Season with pepper and salt.

Spread squash mixture in a baking dish.

Spread mozzarella cheese and ricotta cheese on top.

Select Bake mode.

Set time to 10 minutes and temperature 375 F then press START.

The air fryer display will prompt you to ADD FOOD once the temperature is reached then place the baking dish in the air fryer basket.

Drizzle with basil pesto and serve.

Cauliflower Casserole

Preparation Time: 10 minutes

Cooking Time: 15 minutes

Serve: 6

Ingredients:

1 cauliflower head, cut into florets and boil

1 cup cheddar cheese, shredded

1 cup mozzarella cheese, shredded

2 oz cream cheese

1 cup heavy cream

1/2 tsp pepper

1/2 tsp salt

Directions:

Add cream in a small saucepan and bring to simmer, stir well.

Add cream cheese and stir until thickens.

Remove from heat and add 1 cup shredded cheddar cheese and seasoning and stir well.

Place boiled cauliflower florets into the greased baking dish.

Pour saucepan mixture over cauliflower florets.

Sprinkle mozzarella cheese over the cauliflower mixture.

Select Bake mode.

Set time to 15 minutes and temperature 375 F then press START.

The air fryer display will prompt you to ADD FOOD once the temperature is reached then place the baking dish in the air fryer basket.

Serve and enjoy

Air Fry Green Beans

Preparation Time: 5 minutes

Cooking Time: 10 minutes

Serve: 2

Ingredients:

2 cups green beans

2 tbsp olive oil

1/4 tsp ground coriander

1/4 tsp ground cumin

1/2 tsp dried oregano

1/8 tsp cayenne pepper

1/8 tsp ground allspice

1/4 tsp ground cinnamon

1/2 tsp salt

Directions:

Add all ingredients into the mixing bowl and toss well.

Select Bake mode.

Set time to 10 minutes and temperature 370 F then press START.

The air fryer display will prompt you to ADD FOOD once the temperature is reached then add green beans in the air fryer basket.

Shake basket halfway through Serve and enjoy.

Lemon Green Beans

Preparation Time: 5 minutes

Cooking Time: 10 minutes

Serve: 2

Ingredients:

1lb green beans, washed and ends trimmed

1 fresh lemon juice

1/4 tsp olive oil

Pepper

Salt

Directions:

Place green beans in a baking dish and drizzle with lemon juice and oil.

Season with pepper and salt.

Select Bake mode.

Set time to 10 minutes and temperature 400 F then press START.

The air fryer display will prompt you to ADD FOOD once the temperature is reached then place the baking dish in the air fryer basket.

Serve and enjoy.

Mixed Vegetables

Preparation Time: 10 minutes

Cooking Time: 10 minutes

Serve: 6

Ingredients:

2 cups mushrooms, cut in half

3/4 tsp Italian seasoning

1/2 onion, sliced

1/2 cup olive oil

2 yellow squash, sliced

2 medium zucchini, sliced

1/2 tsp garlic salt

Directions:

Add vegetables and remaining ingredients into the mixing bowl and toss well.

Select Air Fry mode.

Set time to 10 minutes and temperature 400 F then press START.

The air fryer display will prompt you to ADD FOOD once the temperature is reached then add vegetables in the air fryer basket.

Serve and enjoy.

Jicama & Green Beans

Preparation Time: 10 minutes

Cooking Time: 45 minutes

Serve: 6

Ingredients:

1 medium jicama, cubed

12 oz green beans, sliced in half

3 garlic cloves

3 tbsp olive oil

1 tsp dried thyme

1 tsp dried rosemary

1/2 tsp salt

Directions:

Add green beans, jicama, thyme, rosemary, garlic, oil, and salt into the mixing bowl and toss well.

Spread green beans and jicama mixture into a baking dish.

Select Air Fry mode.

Set time to 45 minutes and temperature 400 F then press START.

The air fryer display will prompt you to ADD FOOD once the temperature is reached then place the baking dish in the air fryer basket.

Stir halfway through.

Serve and enjoy.

Squash & Zucchini

Preparation Time: 10 minutes

Cooking Time: 25 minutes

Serve: 4

Ingredients:

1 lb yellow squash, cut into

1/2-inch half-moons

1 lb zucchini, cut into

1/2-inch half-moons

1 tbsp olive oil

Pepper

Salt

Directions:

In a bowl, add zucchini, squash, oil, pepper, and salt and toss well.

Select Bake mode.

Set time to 25 minutes and temperature 400 F then press START.

The air fryer display will prompt you to ADD FOOD once the temperature is reached then add zucchini and squash mixture in the air fryer basket.

Serve and enjoy.

Air Fried Cabbage

Preparation Time: 10 minutes

Cooking Time: 10 minutes

Serve: 2

Ingredients:

1/2 cabbage head, sliced into 2-inch slices

1 tbsp olive oil

1/2 tsp garlic powder

Pepper

Salt

Directions:

Drizzle cabbage with olive oil and season with garlic powder, pepper, and salt.

Select Bake mode.

Set time to 10 minutes and temperature 375 F then press START.

The air fryer display will prompt you to ADD FOOD once the temperature is reached then place Cabbage slices in the air fryer basket.

Turn cabbage slices halfway through.

Serve and enjoy

Crisp & Crunchy Asparagus

Preparation Time: 10 minutes

Cooking Time: 10 minutes

Serve: 4

Ingredients:

1 lb asparagus, trim ends & cut in half

1 tbsp vinegar

2 tbsp coconut aminos

1 tbsp butter, melted

1 tbsp olive oil

1/2 tsp sea salt

Directions:

In a bowl, toss asparagus with olive oil and salt.

Place the cooking tray in the air fryer basket.

Select Air Fry mode.

Set time to 10 minutes and temperature 400 F then press START.

The air fryer display will prompt you to ADD FOOD once the temperature is reached then add asparagus in the air fryer basket.

Meanwhile, for the sauce in a bowl, mix together coconut aminos, melted butter, and vinegar.

Pour sauce over hot asparagus and serve.

Healthy Roasted Vegetables

Preparation Time: 10 minutes

Cooking Time: 14 minutes

Serve: 4

Ingredients:

8 oz asparagus, cut the ends

8 oz mushrooms, halved

1 zucchini, sliced

6 oz grape tomatoes

1/2 tsp pepper

1 tbsp Dijon mustard

1 tbsp soy sauce

1/4 cup balsamic vinegar

4 tbsp olive oil

Directions:

In a large bowl, mix together olive oil, vinegar, soy sauce, Dijon mustard, and pepper.

Add asparagus, tomatoes, zucchini, and mushrooms into the bowl and toss until well coated.

Place vegetables in the refrigerator for 30 minutes.

Place the cooking tray in the air fryer basket.

Select Air Fry mode.

Set time to 14 minutes and temperature 400 F then press START.

The air fryer display will prompt you to ADD FOOD once the temperature is reached then add marinated vegetables in the air fryer basket.

Stir vegetables halfway through.

Serve and enjoy.

Rosemary Basil Mushrooms

Preparation Time: 10 minutes

Cooking Time: 14 minutes

Serve: 4

Ingredients:

1 lb mushrooms

1/2 tbsp vinegar

1/2 tsp ground coriander

1 tsp rosemary, chopped

1 tbsp basil, minced

1 garlic clove, minced

Pepper

Salt

Directions:

Add all ingredients into the large bowl and toss well.

Select Air Fry mode.

Set time to 14 minutes and temperature 350 F then press START.

The air fryer display will prompt you to ADD FOOD once the temperature is reached then add mushrooms in the air fryer basket.

Serve and enjoy.

Old Bay Cauliflower Florets

Preparation Time: 10 minutes

Cooking Time: 15 minutes

Serve: 4

Ingredients:

1 medium cauliflower head, cut into florets

1/2 tsp old bay seasoning

1/4 tsp paprika

1 tbsp garlic, minced

3 tbsp olive oil

Pepper

Salt

Directions:

In a large bowl, toss cauliflower with remaining ingredients.

Select Air Fry mode.

Set time to 15 minutes and temperature 400 F then press START.

The air fryer display will prompt you to ADD FOOD once the temperature is reached then add cauliflower florets in the air fryer basket.

Serve and enjoy.

Air Fry Bell Peppers

Preparation Time: 10 minutes

Cooking Time: 8 minutes

Serve: 3

Ingredients:

1 cup red bell peppers, cut into chunks

1 cup green bell peppers, cut into chunks

1 cup yellow bell peppers, cut into chunks

1 tsp olive oil

1/4 tsp garlic powder

Pepper

Salt

Directions:

Add all ingredients into the large bowl and toss well.

Select Air Fry mode.

Set time to 8 minutes and temperature 360 F then press START.

The air fryer display will prompt you to ADD FOOD once the temperature is reached then add bell peppers in the air fryer basket.

Stir halfway through.

Serve and enjoy.

Mushrooms Cauliflower Roast

Preparation Time: 10 minutes

Cooking Time: 25 minutes

Serve: 6

Ingredients:

1 lb mushrooms, cleaned

10 garlic cloves, peeled

2 cups cherry tomatoes

2 cups cauliflower florets

1 tbsp fresh parsley, chopped

1 tbsp Italian seasoning

2 tbsp olive oil

Pepper

Salt

Directions:

Add cauliflower, mushrooms, Italian seasoning, olive oil, garlic, cherry tomatoes, pepper, and salt into the mixing bowl and toss well.

Transfer cauliflower and mushroom mixture in baking dish.

Select Bake mode.

Set time to 25 minutes and temperature 400 F then press START.

The air fryer display will prompt you to ADD FOOD once the temperature is reached then place the baking dish in the air fryer basket.

Serve and enjoy

Healthy Roasted Broccoli

Preparation Time: 10 minutes

Cooking Time: 20 minutes

Serve: 6

Ingredients:

4 cups broccoli florets

3 tbsp olive oil

1/2 tsp pepper

1/2 tsp garlic powder

1 tsp Italian seasoning

1 tsp salt

Directions:

Add broccoli in a baking dish and drizzle with oil and season with garlic powder, Italian seasoning, pepper, and salt.

Select Bake mode.

Set time to 20 minutes and temperature 400 F then press START.

The air fryer display will prompt you to ADD FOOD once the temperature is reached then place the baking dish in the air fryer basket.

Serve and enjoy.

Crispy Brussels Sprouts

Preparation Time: 10 minutes

Cooking Time: 14 minutes

Serve: 2

Ingredients:

1/2 lb Brussels sprouts, trimmed and halved

1/2 tsp chili powder

1/2 tbsp olive oil

Pepper

Salt

Directions:

Add all ingredients into the large bowl and toss well.

Select Air Fry mode.

Set time to 14 minutes and temperature 350 F then press START.

The air fryer display will prompt you to ADD FOOD once the temperature is reached then add brussels sprouts in the air fryer basket.

Serve and enjoy.

Baked Artichoke Hearts

Preparation Time: 10 minutes

Cooking Time: 25 minutes

Serve: 6

Ingredients:

18 oz frozen artichoke hearts, defrosted

1 tbsp olive oil

Pepper

Salt

Directions:

Brush artichoke hearts with oil and season with pepper and salt.

Select Bake mode.

Set time to 25 minutes and temperature 400 F then press START.

The air fryer display will prompt you to ADD FOOD once the temperature is reached then place artichoke hearts in the air fryer basket. Serve and enjoy.

Lemon Garlic Cauliflower

Preparation Time: 10 minutes

Cooking Time: 35 minutes

Serve: 4

Ingredients:

6 cups cauliflower florets

5 garlic cloves, chopped

1/4 fresh lemon juice

2 tbsp olive oil

1/2 tsp onion powder

1/4 tsp cayenne

Pepper

Salt

Directions:

Add all ingredients into the large bowl and toss well.

Select Roast mode.

Set time to 35 minutes and temperature 400 F then press START.

The air fryer display will prompt you to ADD FOOD once the temperature is reached then add cauliflower florets in the air fryer basket.

Stir halfway through.

Serve and enjoy.

Air Fry Parmesan Tomatoes

Preparation Time: 10 minutes

Cooking Time: 25 minutes

Serve: 4

Ingredients:

4 large tomatoes, halved

2 tbsp parmesan cheese, grated

1 tbsp vinegar

1 tbsp olive oil

1/2 tsp fresh parsley, chopped

1 tsp fresh basil, minced

1 garlic clove, minced

Pepper

Salt

Directions:

In a bowl, mix together oil, basil, garlic, vinegar, pepper, and salt.

Add tomatoes and stir well to coat.

Select Air Fry mode.

Set time to 25 minutes and temperature 320 F then press START.

The air fryer display will prompt you to ADD FOOD once the temperature is reached then place tomato halves in the air fryer basket.

Sprinkle tomatoes with parmesan cheese and cook for 5 minutes more.

Serve and enjoy

Roasted Squash

Preparation Time: 10 minutes

Cooking Time: 60 minutes

Serve: 4

Ingredients:

2 lbs summer squash, cut into 1-inch pieces

1/8 tsp garlic powder

3 tbsp olive oil

1 large lemon

1/8 tsp paprika

1/8 tsp pepper

Pepper

Salt

Directions:

Place squash pieces into the baking dish and drizzle with olive oil.

Season with paprika, pepper, and garlic powder.

Squeeze lemon juice over the squash.

Select Bake mode.

Set time to 60 minutes and temperature 400 F then press START.

The air fryer display will prompt you to ADD FOOD once the temperature is reached then place the baking dish in the air fryer basket.

Serve and enjoy

Parmesan Eggplant Zucchini

Preparation Time: 10 minutes

Cooking Time: 35 minutes

Serve: 6

Ingredients:

1 medium eggplant, sliced

3 medium zucchini, sliced

3 oz Parmesan cheese, grated

1 tbsp olive oil

1 cup cherry tomatoes, halved

4 garlic cloves, minced

4 tbsp parsley, chopped

4 tbsp basil, chopped

1/4 tsp pepper

1/4 tsp salt

Directions:

In a mixing bowl, add chopped cherry tomatoes, eggplant, zucchini, olive oil, garlic, cheese, basil, pepper, and salt toss well until combined.

Transfer the eggplant mixture into the baking dish.

Select Bake mode.

Set time to 35 minutes and temperature 350 F then press START.

The air fryer display will prompt you to ADD FOOD once the temperature is reached then place the baking dish in the air fryer basket.

Serve and enjoy

Lightning Source UK Ltd.
Milton Keynes UK
UKHW020650040123
414807UK00001B/15